EDGE BOOKS™

SUPER TRIVIA COLLECTION

THIS BOOK REQUIRES SAFETY GOGGLES

BY KRISTI LEW

A COLLECTION OF BIZARRE SCIENCE TRIVIA

CAPSTONE PRESS
a capstone imprint

Edge Books are published by Capstone Press,
1710 Roe Crest Drive, North Mankato, Minnesota 56003.
www.capstonepub.com

Books published by Capstone Press are manufactured with paper
containing at least 10 percent post-consumer waste.

Library of Congress Cataloging-in-Publication Data
Lew, Kristi.
  This book requires safety goggles : a collection of bizarre science trivia / by Kristi
Lew.
      p. cm. — (Edge books. Super trivia collection)
  Includes bibliographical references and index.
  Summary: "Describes a variety of trivia facts about science"—Provided by publisher.
  ISBN 978-1-4296-7654-0 (library binding)
  1. Science—Miscellanea. I. Title. II. Series.
  Q173.L576 2012
  500—dc23   2011035737

Editorial Credits

Angie Kaelberer, editor; Alison Thiele, designer; Svetlana Zhurkin, media researcher;
    Laura Manthe, production specialist

Photo Credits

Alamy: Jochen Tack, 17; Capstone Studio: Karon Dubke, 19 (bottom); CDC: Brian Judd, 22
(top); Corbis: Raymond Gehman, 24 (top); Digital Vision, 14 (top); Dreamstime: Christos
Georghiou, 28 (top), Mrcq4, 24 (bottom); iStockphoto: Terry Wilson, 27 (top); NASA,
26 (bottom), JPL/University of Arizona (Jupiter), 27 (bottom); National Park Service,
U.S. Department of the Interior, 9 (top); Newscom: RTR/Richard Carson, 20 (middle);
Shutterstock: 26kot (water), 12 (bottom), Aaron Amat, 15 (top), AISPIX, 25 (top), Aliaksei
Hintau, 16 (right), Andrea Danti, 26 (top), Anthonycz, 6 (bottom front), Armin Rose, 8 (top),
Aromant, 10 (bottom left), Cory Thoman, 10 (bottom right), Creatista, 20 (bottom), Denis
Vrublevski, 13 (middle), Derek Gordon, cover (bottom right), Dmitriy Shironosov, 23 (middle),
DVARG, 10 (top), Fernando Cortes (background), throughout, FloridaStock, 6 (top), Galyna
Andrushko, 8 (bottom), George Dolgikh, cover (middle left), 1 (bottom), hd connelly, 25
(bottom), Igor Chaikovskiy (Earth), 27 (middle left), indiwarm, 16 (left), Janne Hämäläinen, 9
(bottom), jannoon028, 23 (bottom), JustASC, 19 (top), Kacso Sandor, 22 (bottom), Laurence
Gough, 4–5, 29, Marcel Clemens, 1 (middle left), 3 (bottom), 13 (bottom), Marie C. Fields,
13 (top), Marinko Tarlac, cover (bottom left), mmutlu, 21 (bottom), nenadv, 23 (top), Oleksiy
Mark, 15 (middle), Olga Miltsova, 14 (bottom), olly, 28 (bottom), Omelchenko, 6 (bottom
back), Rafael Pacheco (Moon), 27 (middle right), Sebastian Kaulitzki, 21 (top), serazetdinov,
18 (bottom), unkreativ, 15 (bottom), vicspacewalker, 7 (top), vitek12, 11 (top), yuri4u80, 11
(bottom), Zeljko Radojko, 18 (top), zentilia (gold), 12 (middle); Wikimedia: Stubb, 7 (bottom)

Printed in the United States of America in Stevens Point, Wisconsin.
102011   006404WZS12

TABLE OF CONTENTS

WACKY WORLD OF SCIENCE

➡ You had more bones when you were born than you do now.

➡ Astronauts get taller in space.

➡ Table salt is formed by a reaction between a metal and a poisonous gas.

These pieces of information may sound like science fiction, but they're really science fact. Let's explore the explanations for these facts and many others. Welcome to the wonderful, wild, wacky world of science!

Chapter 1

EXTREME EARTH

Earth can be a pretty strange place. Think all deserts are hot? Think again. Let's explore wild facts about our amazing planet.

You know that ocean water contains salt, right? But did you know that if all the salt in the ocean was removed and spread evenly over Earth's land surface, it would be more than 500 feet (152 meters) thick? That's about the height of a 50-story building!

Have you ever heard someone say, "that will knock your socks off"? A lightning strike can actually knock a person's shoes and socks off! As lightning travels across the body's surface, damp skin in the path of the current produces high-pressure steam. This can knock off shoes and socks!

It's easy to float in the Dead Sea—people just bob on top of the water like a cork. Water in the Dead Sea has about six times more salt in it than any other saltwater body of water. All this salt makes the water **denser** than the human body, allowing you to float freely.

Look out below!

The Cave of Swallows in San Luis Potosi, Mexico, is deep enough to hold the 102-story Empire State Building. With a vertical drop of 1,220 feet (372 m), this cave is one of the deepest on Earth. In fact, it is so deep that explorers sometimes parachute to the bottom!

density—how heavy or light an object is for its size

Not all deserts are hot. Freezing cold Antarctica is Earth's largest desert. Deserts get less than 10 inches (25 centimeters) of **precipitation** a year. Antarctica averages about 2 inches (5 cm) of snowfall a year. This makes the cold continent drier than the blazing hot Sahara Desert, which gets 3 inches (7.6 cm) of rain each year.

People spend about a quarter of their lives growing. But did you know that mountains also grow? Mount Everest is the world's tallest mountain. It is getting taller every year! Earth's crust is broken into chunks called plates. These plates slowly move and crash into each other. These collisions push Mount Everest upward by about 0.2 inch (5 millimeters) a year.

precipitation—water that falls from clouds to Earth's surface

Volcanoes often form slowly. But one was in a hurry to grow up! On February 20, 1943, the ground opened near the village of Paricutin, Mexico. Hot rocks shot from the opening. By the end of the day, the new volcano was 35 feet (11 m) high. By 1952 it measured 1,391 feet (424 m) and had destroyed two towns.

Did you know waterfalls flow beneath the sea? These waterfalls are called cataracts. The largest cataract is between Greenland and Iceland. It drops nearly 11,500 feet (3,505 m). This is more than three times the length of Angel Falls in Venezuela, Earth's highest above-ground waterfall.

Angel Falls ★

Ocean waves need wind or storms to develop, right? Not so fast. Rogue waves up to 100 feet (30 m) tall can form in calm water. These waves form when several smaller waves come together at the same moment.

If you've ever been around a natural gas leak, you've probably held your nose. The gas smells like rotten eggs! But natural gas really has no odor. Leaking natural gas explodes very easily. Gas companies add chemicals to make the gas smell bad. People then recognize the odor and get to safety.

GAS

GAS

What makes the White Cliffs of Dover, England, so white? Chalk! Chalk is made up of skeletons of trillions of **plankton**. As the plankton died, they settled to the bottom of the ocean. Heat and pressure turned the layers of skeletons into rock. Movements of Earth's plates shoved the rock upward, making it dry land.

Lightning strikes the Earth more than 8 million times a day. The air around a lightning bolt can be as hot as 50,000 degrees Fahrenheit (27,760 degrees Celsius). Southwestern Florida has an average of 100 days with thunderstorms each year. This makes it the U.S. lightning capital!

plankton—single-celled plants and animals that live in water

Chapter 2
CRAZY CHEMISTRY

Did you know that every day you eat a chemical made from an exploding metal and a poisonous gas? Or that regular household vinegar could destroy your mother's favorite pearl necklace? Keep reading to learn how all this crazy chemistry works.

The ocean is filled with trace elements of gold. If all of that gold was removed from the ocean, every person on Earth could receive 9 pounds (4 kilograms) of the precious metal!

What could a diamond and your pencil possibly have in common? The writing material in a pencil is graphite. Graphite and diamonds are both made of carbon, but they are very different. Graphite is a soft, dull gray mineral. Diamonds are glittery, hard, and clear. These differences are caused by how the carbon atoms are arranged.

Most metals are hard and cool to the touch. But the metal mercury is liquid at room temperature and standard atmospheric pressure. Mercury was once used in thermometers to measure temperature. Now it's used mainly in scientific research and electricity production.

atom—an element in its smallest form

Do rocks float on water? Pumice does. Pumice is formed when **lava** comes into contact with water. The rapid cooling of the hot lava creates bubbles as it turns the lava into solid rock. The bubbles in the rock make it less dense and allow the dry rock to float on water.

Get out of my way!

Want to make a pearl necklace disappear? Pour vinegar on it! Vinegar is an acid. Pearls are made of calcium carbonate. When these two substances mix, a chemical reaction occurs. The reaction dissolves the pearl and releases **carbon dioxide**. Small pearls measuring 0.33 inch (8.4 mm) can dissolve in just 72 hours.

lava—hot, liquid rock from a volcano
carbon dioxide—a colorless, odorless gas

What do you get when a metal that explodes in water and a yellow-green poisonous gas chemically react with one another? Something you use every day—ordinary table salt. The chemical name for table salt is sodium chloride. In its pure form, sodium is a metal that reacts violently with water. Chlorine is a poisonous gas. But when they chemically react with one another, they make harmless table salt.

The periodic table of elements includes the 118 known chemical elements. Each element has a one- or two-letter abbreviation, but two letters aren't found. What are they? J and Q.

Chapter 3
FANTASTIC PHYSICS

What do floating frogs, cow manure, and air pressure all have in common? They're all involved in some fantastic physics facts.

If you have a powerful magnet, you can make a frog float on air! Like everything else in the world, frogs are made up of atoms. Atoms are made up of smaller units called electrons, protons, and neutrons. When an atom is put into a very strong magnetic field, the electrons in the atom shift their position slightly. This shift gives the atoms their own magnetic fields. The magnetic field of the frog's atoms and the external magnetic field **repel** each other. This causes the frog to **levitate**.

Let's float!

repel—to push apart
levitate—to rise into the air and float

Water can't cut through steel, can it? It can if the water pressure is great enough. Water jets with pressures between 20,000 and 55,000 pounds per square inch (138 million and 379 million pascals) easily cut through steel up to 2 inches (5 cm) thick. A fine dusting of the gem garnet is added to the water jet to help it cut through the metal.

OUTRAGEOUS
BIZARRE SCIENCE
TRIVIA

Microwave Magic

Something you probably use every day in your kitchen got its start spying for the military! In World War II (1939–1945), British scientists invented magnetron tubes, which produce microwaves. The tubes were installed in radar detectors to spot German airplanes. But that's not the end of the microwave's story. In 1946 scientist Percy Spencer was testing the magnetron tube when he realized that the tube's waves had melted a candy bar in his pocket. He then tested the microwaves to see if they would pop popcorn. They did—and the microwave oven was born. These early ovens were about the size of a refrigerator and sold for $5,000!

Farmers in Vermont are turning cow manure into power. The Audet family of rural Bridport, Vermont, owns more than 1,000 cows. Those cows produce a lot of manure. The Audets collect the poop in a big tank called a digester. There, **bacteria** break down the manure, producing methane gas. This gas is used as a fuel to make electricity. The Audets' cows produce enough poop to power about 400 homes!

Three cheers for poop power!

Air doesn't weigh anything, does it? Wrong! Air pressure is created by compressed air **molecules**. About 1 ton (0.9 metric ton) of air pressure is on you at all times. That's about the weight of a small car!

bacteria—microscopic living things
molecule—two or more atoms that have bonded

Baseball fans know that a curveball is often harder to hit than a straight pitch. The curveball's spinning motion is the secret of its success. The spinning motion makes air flow differently over the top of the ball than it does under the ball. The air under the ball flows faster than the air on top of the ball. This forces the ball to move down or curve. This imbalance of force is called the Magnus Effect.

A substance can't be both a solid and a liquid at the same time, can it? It can if it's a mixture of cornstarch and water. Some people call the mixture oobleck. Oobleck acts like a solid when pressure is applied on it. Once the pressure is released, it flows like a liquid.

Chapter 4

BIZARRE BIOLOGY

Did you know that you're not alone in your body? Or that a sneeze can spray snot as fast as a speeding car can travel? Plants, animals, and humans are sources of amazing facts.

Eww, nasty!

Houston Museum of natural science

Not all flowers smell sweet. The titan arum, or corpse flower, actually smells like rotting flesh! The plant's stalk can reach 10 feet (3 m) tall. The flowers are 3 to 4 feet (0.9 to 1.2 m) wide. The plant can live many years without producing a flower. But once the flower blooms, plug your nose! People can smell its horrible odor 0.5 mile (0.8 kilometer) away.

Like fingerprints, everyone's tongue print is unique.

It's hard to believe, but most of the cells in your body don't even belong to you. The bacteria living in your body outnumbers your cells by 10 to 1! Some of the bacteria are helpful, but others can cause disease.

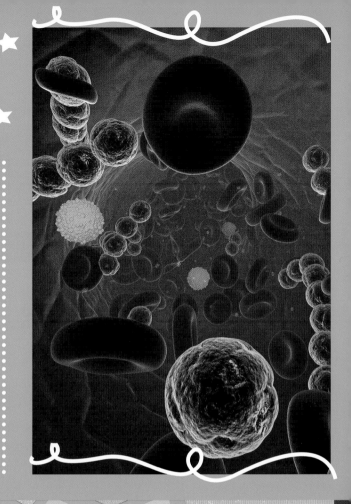

liver ★

The liver is the only human organ that can **regenerate** itself. A person can give part of his or her liver to another person, and the liver will grow back!

regenerate—to grow again

There's a good reason to cover your mouth when you sneeze. A sneeze can blast out of your nose and mouth at 100 miles (161 km) per hour! The spray can spread out 5 feet (1.5 m).

Do your feet stink when you take off your shoes? Your feet have more sweat glands than any other part of your body. Between the two of them, they have about 500,000 sweat glands. But that's not why feet stink. Sweat is basically water and salt. It doesn't smell at all. But bacteria love to munch on salty sweat, and they produce waste. This waste creates a smell that will clear a room when you kick off your shoes!

Have you ever had glowing red eyes on a photo? Don't worry—you're not turning into a werewolf. The pupil of your eye is just an opening that lets light into the eye. The flash of a camera can send light into the pupil and light up the retina on the inside of the eye. Retinas are mostly red. So the red-eye in the photo is actually a picture of the inside of your eye!

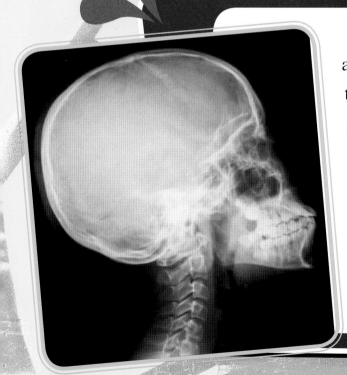

You were born with about 300 bones. By the time you're an adult, you'll only have 206. How can that be? Some bones fuse as you get older. These bones include those of the skull and the base of the spine.

fuse—to join together

Is it getting hot in here?

The bark of a giant sequoia tree wouldn't make good firewood—it's fire-resistant! The spongy bark on these mature redwoods can be more than 2 feet (0.6 m) thick. The bark's thickness and the amount of water it contains help protect the trees from forest fires.

Can something that's been frozen for millions of years come back to life? Scientists have successfully revived 8-million-year-old bacteria found under ice in Antarctica. Once thawed, the bacteria went back to doing what bacteria do—reproducing.

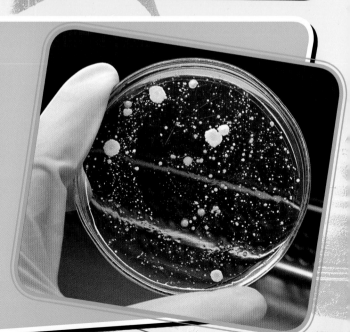

Ever tried to have a stare-down with a baby? Infants blink only once or twice a minute. Adults blink an average of 10 times per minute. Babies' eyelid openings are smaller in relation to the eye. So a baby's eyes may not become dry as quickly as an adult's.

Stare me down! I dare you!

Why do your fingers and toes wrinkle after a long soak in the bathtub or swimming pool? You have extra amounts of dead skin on your fingers and toes. This dead skin absorbs water. It then wrinkles as it expands in size.

Chapter 5

OUT OF THIS WORLD

These out-of-this-world facts come from outside Earth's atmosphere. Learn about Earth's growing weight problem and how to make Saturn float.

If you had a swimming pool that was 75,000 miles (120,700 km) wide, you could float Saturn in it! Saturn is made up mainly of hydrogen and helium. It is the least dense of all the planets. With a density less than that of water, Saturn could float.

Astronauts can be up to 2 inches (5 cm) taller in space. There is less gravity in space than there is on Earth. This allows the bones in the astronauts' backbones to stretch out, making them taller. Once they return to Earth's gravity, they return to their normal height.

Does Earth need to go on a diet? Earth gains weight every day from meteorites and other debris falling from space. Scientists estimate that Earth gains 37,000 to 78,000 tons (33,565 to 70,760 metric tons) per year.

Your weight doesn't change if you travel, right? Not so fast! If you weigh 100 pounds (45 kg) on Earth, you would weigh only 17 pounds (8 kg) on the moon. On Jupiter, you'd weigh 236 pounds (107 kg). No matter where you go in the universe, you have the same amount of mass. But your weight depends on gravity. On planets that have less gravity than Earth, you weigh less. On planets with more gravity, you weigh more.

meteorite—a piece of rock from space

mass—the amount of matter someone or something has

The closer you are to the Sun, the hotter you are, right? Not always! Even though Mercury is the closest planet to the Sun, Venus is the hottest planet in our solar system. Venus' dense atmosphere contains both sulfuric acid and carbon dioxide, which help trap the Sun's heat. The temperature on Venus is about 870°F (465°C).

Venus ★

Is there sound in space? Actually, no. Sound waves need to travel through a medium, such as air or water. Space is a vacuum containing no molecules, so the sound waves don't travel.

SEEING IS BELIEVING

The bizarre world of science reaches far beyond your school's laboratory. Why stop now? Keep your eyes and ears open for more wild and wonderful facts about the world of science!

GLOSSARY

atom (AT-uhm)—an element in its smallest form

bacteria (bak-TEER-ee-uh)—microscopic living things; some bacteria cause disease

carbon dioxide (KAHR-buhn dy-AHK-syde)—a colorless, odorless gas that people and animals breathe out

density (DEN-si-tee)—how heavy or light an object is for its size

fuse (FYOOZ)—to join together

lava (LAH-vuh)—the hot, liquid rock that pours out of a volcano when it erupts

levitate (LEV-i-tate)—to rise in the air and float

mass (MASS)—the amount of matter a person or an object has

meteorite (MEE-tee-ur-rite)—a piece of rock from space that strikes a planet or a moon

molecule (MOL-uh-kyool)—two or more atoms of the same or different elements that have bonded

plankton (PLANGK-tuhn)—single-celled plants and animals that live in water

precipitation (pri-sip-i-TAY-shuhn)—water that falls from clouds to Earth's surface

regenerate (re-JEN-uh-rayt)—to grow again

repel (ri-PEL)—to push apart

READ MORE

National Geographic Society, ed. *Weird but True! 2: 300 Outrageous Facts.* National Geographic Kids. Washington, D.C.: National Geographic, 2010.

Perritano, John. *Big Book of Why.* New York: Time for Kids Books, 2010.

Ripley Entertainment, ed. *Wonders of Science.* Ripley's Believe It or Not! Broomall, Pa.: Mason Crest, 2009.

INTERNET SITES

FactHound offers a safe, fun way to find Internet sites related to this book. All of the sites on FactHound have been researched by our staff.

Here's all you do:

Visit *www.facthound.com*

Type in this code: 9781429676540

Super-cool stuff! Check out projects, games and lots more at **www.capstonekids.com**

INDEX